I0147537

Dartmouth College

Exercises of class day of the senior class

Tuesday, June 23, 1891

Dartmouth College

Exercises of class day of the senior class
Tuesday, June 23, 1891

ISBN/EAN: 9783337274702

Printed in Europe, USA, Canada, Australia, Japan

Cover: Foto ©Paul-Georg Meister /pixelio.de

More available books at **www.hansebooks.com**

EXERCISES

—OF—

CLASS DAY,

—AT—

DARTMOUTH COLLEGE,

TUESDAY, JUNE 23, 1891.

HANOVER, N. H. :
PUBLISHED BY THE CLASS.
1891.

INTRODUCTORY ADDRESS.

EDMUND JONATHAN BUGBEE, HARTFORD. VT.

ON this day, which is so peculiarly ours, and which is to begin those exercises that are to sever our connections with the College, it is fitting that we review with our Chronicler our association during the past four years, and with the Prophet take a look into the future.

We have now reached that goal in our college course to which we have looked forward so anxiously during the past four years. In two days and we shall have accomplised the greatest work of our lives. It is a turning point that should be well considered. Surely the day should be for us the beginning of a new life, when we should cease looking backward and press on to the things that are before. Our opportunities here may not have been well improved, but neglected opportunities should not be the pattern of our lives. Our college course may not have tended so much to store us with knowledge as to train the mind to act, fitting us for the positions we soon are called on to fill, and helping us to forge that position we would fill among our fellowmen.

Here, during the past four years, secluded from the world without, we have developed within us those principles which shall give direction and character to all our future progress and shall be the stepping stones to our success. With what care these foundations of our future life have been laid the past furnishes no criterion of judgment. However flattering a future our prophet shall assign us to-day, let not his imagination shape our course. The struggle is a even one for most of us, and we may be victorious and successful if we will.

> " Let no one look at fortune cast you down ;
> She were not fortune did she not frown :
> Such as do braveliest bear her scorn awhile
> Are those on whom at last she most will smile."

We will soon find ourselves in the midst of the stream which is dragging us out into the wide world, and like the stream of water which forces for itself a path through difficult passes, so we, with strong and earnest endeavor and by true manhood, must make our path through the difficulties and problems of life. Our success can be achieved only by our own energy and labor.

The fields of labor that lie spread out before us are various. Wherever that field lies, be it in business, profession, or politics, there is a special opportunity for each one of us, and it is a duty that we owe, both to the state and society, that we shall improve the opportunities that have here been given us in the uplifting and enlightenment of our fellowmen. Not for fame. We should look about us for some other motive than the approbation of men. Courage and will are necessary. None of us should shrink from the struggle. Let us so work that the same honor and respect which have been so closely allied with Dartmouth in the past, shall continue to be associated with it wherever the name shall be heard.

To the Alumni, who have come here to revisit their *Alma Mater* and pay their respects to old Dartmouth, and who have already entered upon their life work, seting a mark for us as Dartmouth men to strive for, we extend a cordial welcome.

To our friends, who have made a special effort to be with us this week, who have watched with such care our progress, who have shared with us our joys and triumphs, and who have deemed it a duty and a pleasure to help and guide us, we extend a most hearty welcome, trusting that their efforts in our behalf, and the confidence they have placed in us will not have been in vain.

ORATION.

HERMAN HOWARD KIBBEY, NEWPORT, N. H.

O-DAY we are called to a new experience; we look toward the threshold of the door of departure. Some of our number, it may be, are able to catch glimpses of the imaginary and even the real scenes beyond this threshold. To others, the busy world, the seething, foaming mass of humanity, appears to convey a mysterious language like the ceaseless roaring of the billowy deep, enshrouded in the darkness of night.

We are necessarily impelled, in taking our next advancing step, to lay hold upon the knowledge and experience of others, and joining to this our own limited experience and reflections, to formulate a new vision of life, and it is of the revelation of this vision of humanity that I wish to speak to-day.

An eminent American statesman has given utterance to these expressive words: "Human life! how inspiring, how boundless the theme!" How little in those words, and yet how much! We see them written in bold characters at every milestone, at every turning point of our course. They express, though they do not explain, the relationship between mind and matter. Those words express the condition of every age, of every station of life, of every nationality. They show to us that human life has the same indisputable characteristics the world over, that it involves the soul and the body, it includes the rich and poor, the ignorant and enlightened, the poor wreck of humanity and the pure and noble life whose whole soul is teeming with goodness and radiates with exceeding brilliancy an almost divine inspiration.

The poet, with sad and melancholy strains, has sung of humanity, and ever and anon there come floating out to us the sweet refrains of the bard as a witness of its beauty and grandeur. Patiently has the historian described its beginning, its progress, its deviations and attractions. The wise man has pointed out its errors and layed down principles of reform. The philosopher has drawn out the true ideal of life, declaring general truths, while the painter has vividly portrayed the real, picturing, as he has, the diverse conditions of actual life.

There is a something in relation to this life that is marvelous, almost unutterable. The mother bends o'er the cradle of the infant with a beating, anxious heart. Two different phases present themselves, the deep and tender love of the mother and the expressions of joy and sorrow of the child. Upon the face of that child we see inefaceably stamped the word, *Humanity.* There is the same will, the same intelligence, though like the tiny physical organs undeveloped. But the Power that gave that bit of life may come to demand it again. Then two other phases demand our attention. The one is the bitter anguish of the mother, into whose heart is branded a never healing wound. The other is our involuntary speculation as to the sequel of the departed life.

Again we see the word *Humanity* written upon the face of the youth in joys more gladly experienced and in sorrows more keenly felt. There is an equal development of the mental and the physical. There are the outcroppings of good and evil which appear as harbingers of honor and disgrace.

We see that human impression stamped upon the care-worn brow of the man of middle life. The intellectual capacity has reached its zenith. Thought is no longer mere fanciful impulse but serious, reflective. speculative. The problems of life become food for contemplation. We find the theoretical and the practical man. We find men of all temperaments, dispositions and characters. But however diverse these may be, man is ever human and subject to the wonderful laws that govern humanity.

Once more the human claim asserts itself, as we look upon the aged one, whose locks the cares of many winters have whitened. We painfully watch the tottering steps and listen to the broken phrases, intermingled with sighings for the irretrievable past, the irredeemable lost. How human! How characteristic of our own individual selves.

But through the theatre of this life, where sit the young and old, the fiery steeds of mortality come dashing on, while the scythe-armed chariot mows down its victims without discrimination. We are called from our occupations to gather round the bier, to take a last look at one who, like ourselves, was human, but ah! how changed! The same form is there, but so different we scarcely recognize it. That voice so sweet will never call us again. Those expressions of love and sympathy, so dear to us, are silenced forever. We cry out in the anguish of our hearts, "O grave, where is thy victory?" Our emotions, hitherto bound fast within their prison walls, burst forth like a mighty army.

It is a phenomenon affecting both the mental and the physical, and it draws out the wonderful sympathy of the one for the other. We look upon the inanimate objects about us, but they notice us not; they are cold and unsympathetic. We live on only to find that

> " Evening must usher night,
> Night urge the morrow,
> Month follow month with woe
> And year wake year to sorrow."

But we are inclined to maintain that sorrow is not conducive to man's welfare, that it is an unnatural visitation of evil. It is said that man is created to be happy, and the truth of this assertion is based upon the recognition of his natural desires and the evident manifestations of divine wisdom. We may reach two degrees of happiness, a negative and a positive. By the former we reach the condition of exemption from suffering. The perfection of this state is seen in the life of the animal, bounded by the present, with no thought of the future, and dying without regret. But for man this mere negative happiness is not sufficient.

As the water-lily opens its petals to receive the warm influence of the sun's rays, so do our mental faculties, through perception and reason reach out after those things that afford delight to the senses. Fortunate man, we say, if the fruit of this search shall not result in vain projects or fanciful illusions. Though the object of man's desire may seem to recede in proportion to his advance in the struggle to attain it, though his memory brings suffering from the past, and gathers suffering from the future, his mental excellence is not disproved.

Nature has decreed that the different senses we possess should be to us a source of pleasure. But if our single aim is toward mere physical gratification we cannot reach true happiness. This can only be accomplished as we associate our pleasures with the mind and such happiness can only be perfected according to the moral support which the mind receives.

A beautiful saying is this, that our pleasures become celestial when they connect the past with the present, the present with the future, and the whole with heaven.

But there are gifts which create within the hearts of men something nobler and grander than sensuous satisfactions. These can be seen embellishing the ties of the family, of friendship and society. Among these gifts we note, as especially prominent, filial affection, love, piety and parental tenderness. These sentiments may coexist, thus invigorating one another. They have ever been approved by reason and may be preserved by virtue.

It is by the cultivation of the intellect that we reach higher and grasp more firmly not simply the ideal truth, but the real verities of mortal and immortal existence. A man so developed may bid defiance to the proud world, he cares not for fleeting time or boundless space; it is truth he seeks and truth that he ultimately gains.

The casual observer must exclaim : " Man, thou happily en. dowed and abundantly blessed ! Surely thou must be an appreciative creature ! " Enviable picture, but ah ! We fail to realize the charms of the situations through which we pass. The happy period of our lives is that which is no more.

To the youth time presents a long perspective of which the point of convergence can with difficulty be detected. The sorrows of this period are like warm spring showers, the traces of which have been removed by a gentle breeze. With advancing years the converging point comes nearer and nearer, and the imprint of solicitude can with greater difficulty be effaced.

The poet has truly said, " Man is of few days and full of trouble. He cometh like the flower, and is cut down ; he wasteth away ; he giveth up the ghost, and where is he ? " A question is this that concerns you and me. Can we hope to receive answer to our query ? All nature comes to our assistance. An array of moralists is at hand. The tender plant, whose verdant foliage is blighted by the autumnal frosts, is an emblem of life which conveys to our minds the truth of the inevitable. The seasons, disclosing wonders and demanding reflection, are moralists. The history of the past, the daily occurrences of society, are replete with moral reflections. But the greatest moral teacher that we have is death. Though it places heavily its icy hand upon us, it is but a fulfilment of nature's law, all in all, a desirable end.

It is to this seemingly cruel agent that those affections which give value to life owe their existence. It is that agent that removes the sorrows and ills peculiarly human.

"Man giveth up the ghost and where is he?" The material physical returns to the cold earth, but where is that intellectual that could comprehend the works of God and receive inspiring influence from the Divinity that pervades all nature? Where is the human soul, with its attributes of reason, freedom and moral responsibility? Where is all that is noble, pure and good in human character? Surely, thought and feeling can never be regarded as the product of matter. Where, then, shall we seek them when the body shall have become disorganized and loose the bonds that keep the soul from its upward flight?

There is an eye, it is the eye of faith, that may penetrate the realms of the immortal. Assisted by the moral agencies of nature and following the light of the gospel of Christ this eye of faith may rest in delighted vision upon the glories of the righteous dead.

In conclusion, I would say, let it be the highest aim and never ceasing concern of each one of us assembled here to-day to so live that unnumbered voices of the future generations shall testify to the cherished recollections of our worthy and blameless lives.

POEM.

———

HERBERT SALISBURY HOPKINS, MILLBURY, MASS.

———

TO him who journeys through a lonely land,
Footsore and weary, seeking welcome rest,
A speck of light seen far adown his way
Lightens his footsteps, renews his zeal and zest.

He hurries, stumbli g mayhap in eager haste,
Nowise deterred by fog or mist or rain ;
Counting the labor small, the reward how great,
When he has reached the haven he would gain.

We, too, have travelled far and seen the light
Far in the distance, bright and brighter gleam,
As on and on we strove, and nearer saw
The way of life, spread out as in a dream.

To us come sadder thoughts, for each one knows
That soon must part the ties so strongly wrought;
The friendships, kept through good report and ill:
Fades soon each scene with happy memories fraught.

We laugh, but smiles conceal a bitter pain,
A sudden pang; a sharp swift dart of woe;
We bid a fond good-bye, and turn to hide a tear
When at the last our nearest friend must go.

We linger long to bid the last farewells;
Turn back and backwards, once and still again
To see once more the old familiar scenes,
And taste of sadness that *is* akin to pain.

Slowly sinks the scorching summer sun,
And hides his face behind the veil of night;
We gaze, nor think to see the same again,
As if 'twere hid forever from our sight.

We see the gleaming, starry hosts of heaven
Come one by one to marshal on their nightly plain.

We see the cold and silent moon sail high
In the fleecy clouds like a barque on the stormy main.

We cannot know, we can only feel
That the things of earth and air
Will know our woe and work our weal,
And bestow their kindest care.

And we know that the scenes we have loved so well
When the day was warm and the sun shone bright,
Will forever in our memories dwell
When winter comes, and cheerless night.

And we know, not only things, but men
Will abide in our hearts for many a year,
When we turn from the cares of life again
To think of the faces we once knew here.

And that which we once counted ill,
When seen by retrospection's light,
Perhaps e'en this, to remember will
Be pleasing; time will purge the sight,
And things now hid shall be made clear,
And night no longer hold her sway
Over hearts oppressed by doubt and fear.
On them shall burst a glorious day,
And the clouds of gloom be swept away.

But classmates, while we gather here
Let's give no place for gloom or weeping;
Let us be gay and have good cheer,
While to its close the day is creeping.

Heed thou time's flight; within the glass
The restless sands are swiftly falling.
Seize on the moments as they pass;
A chance once gone is past recalling.

Be strong; go forth into the fight
With all your armor buckled on.
Faint not; look up and see the light
That crowns success and duty done.

Oh Sons of Dartmouth, never doubt nor fear;
The victory's yours, if ye but labor with a will;
Press forward 'till ye reach the often longed for goal;
Let "onward" be your watchword; onward and forward still.

May fortune crown your after years with peace,
And sure success come following in its turn;
May all your days be blessed, and with it all
May these last scenes within your memory burn.

And now the last farewells; the solemn time
When you and I and all of us must part.
The race is run and finished; let us go now
Where duty calls us, into the unknown beyond,
Trusting but still afraid; bold and strong of heart.

ADDRESS TO THE PRESIDENT.

GUY GEORGE, MERIDEN, N. H.

MUCH honored and highly respected President :—In assuming the duties of this portion of our closing exercises, I fully realize my inability to express all that might properly be said on this occasion ; any extended remarks from me would, doubtless, result in your being convinced that this honor was assigned not for any special merit of my own. but because I alone best represent the *bulk* of the class. It is with peculiar pleasure that we stand before you to-day. We are truly glad to be here, so near reaching that to which we have been looking forward : yes, with some of us it is what we have been fighting for since first we were thrilled with a feeling of profound respect for any person who had been through college. Yet the thought that these pleasant associations are soon to be among things past, and known to us only in remembrance, renders our pleasure indeed a peculiar one : but for us now to hesitate to seek new fields of action would be cowardice; it would seem that we—notwithstanding your own and your associates, efforts—have failed to obtain the object sought in this course ; but happily such is not the case, for that same ambition that brought us here has, by your careful guidance, been directed and strengthened so that we are now ambitious to go forth not as ordinary men, but as good representatives of Old Dartmouth.

We expect to find that this world is a largish place, and no one of us may yet hope to turn everything inside out; but suppose some of us are destined to be reckoned with the many who live for naught, get checked in every great effort, toil with brain and limb for things that have no more to do with a manly life than tarts and confectionery, we shall still praise our *Alma Mater* for what she did for us and never blame *her* for what we are not.

And, Sir, it is with a deep sense of gratitude as well as gratification that we recall your efforts to secure for us a pleas-

ant and instructive course ; that same spirit of personal interest,
manifest even in your correspondence, which aided some of us
to choose this in preference to any other institution, has seemed
to increase throughout our sojourn here, thus making the ties
that bind us ever stronger.   Well do we remember the time
when, early in our course, you were absent ; how much you were
missed ; and on your return, how we hailed your arrival with
pride and pleasure.

In glancing back over these four years we see many places
where, could we but retrace our steps, we would do differently,
nor do we expect to pass any considerable portion of our allot-
ted period without stumbling more or less by the way ; yet we
may be able, by our own blunders, to help smooth the path for
those who come after us in this course.   It is true that we mor-
tals sometimes cut a pitiable figure in our attempts at display :
we may feel sure of our merit, yet be totally ignorant of the
point of view from which we are regarded by our neighbor.   Perhaps we have been a greater cause of annoyance to you than
some other classes—possibly thirteen is rightly considered an
unlucky number, if so, the fact that there are seven thirteens in
ninety-one may explain many things otherwise unaccountable—
however, we would not seem to make this a time of reckoning.
Your efforts have ever been for our greatest good ; unselfish and
painstaking, you have, by your own example and teachings,
pointed out to us a manly, moral and religious life, such as is
not to be surpassed in excellence.   We shall carry away only
memories of the pleasantest acquaintance and relation ; and
wherever we may be we shall frequently be here in spirit, in
this college, whose life we have come to make almost a part of
ourselves.

You can never know how much you have done for us : as
the slightest breeze on yonder mountain top may determine
whether a drop shall reach the Atlantic by the Connecticut or
the Hudson, so may the whole course of our career be changed
by some trifling affair, and when we consider *you* and your position, we can but congratulate you on the great work you have
done and are doing here.   Surely if, as it is written, we are to
be judged in the hereafter by our deeds here, your reward will
not be small.

We could not depart without saying a word to those who have been our instructors. We realize that hardly too much credit can be given them for the kind interest they have ever manifested in our welfare. We wish to thank them for their forbearance and for their friendly disposition ever manifested toward us; in fact, if I may be allowed to use a figure old but still true, our college life seems analogous to a voyage on board a pleasant sailing vessel —not without some storms, to be sure, in which a few of our number were washed overboard, while others of us have had some hard struggles with certain tidal-wave examinations; yet. as we stand here and look back we can truly say we have had a pleasant and profitable voyage, for which to you and your associates we cannot be too grateful. Many of us know what it is to separate from a home, on which we had depended for counsel and example, and start to battle life's journey alone; it is with such feelings that we set forth from our dear old *Alma Mater*. You have done your duty toward moulding and fixing our character, the result rests with ourselves.

CAMPUS ORATION.

FRANK ELEAZER ROWE, WINCHESTER, MASS.

CLASSMATES :—'Tis a sad duty we have to perform when now we bid farewell to this spot, which has been to us the source of more pleasure than any other ground. Four years we have actively engaged in various games on this field, and not one of us, as he looks back on those happy years, can fail to catch glimpses of scenes which will ever remain in the mind as only such scenes can.

What little cause for wonder there is that we should so enjoy ourselves on this campus! Where can anyone point out a more beautiful green for our sports? With the splendid fringe of trees, and situated in the heart of the village, a natural stopping place, little can we wonder that our feet have loved to linger here so much.

What little need have I to rehearse to you a history of the doings of '91 on this field. How often have we discussed the victories and defeats, but, unlike other happenings, there is a pleasure in talking of recollections of the campus drawn from no other source. Here we have vied with each other, with other classes, and with other colleges. Sometimes Defeat has remained with us, but with strong, united efforts have we risen to thrust her forth. Victory we have sought and cherished, and with what pangs have we seen her depart, and then with what resolute hearts we resolved to again entice her to our midst!

I remember with peculiar clearness our first victory on this field, when from their uneasy positions our victorious tug-of-war looked down upon their living seats howling like demons to offset the hollow groans of '90.

In base-ball we never were noted, principally because our players would leave at inopportune moments; freshman year it was impossible to successfully compete with the veteran seniors, and when we gained experience we lost our strength.

We entered Hanover unheralded as wonderful athletes, but, how long will the memory of one or two of our number survive ! Nobody can forget that throw made by a '91 man !

We cannot, as a class, look upon many championships, but as we reflect that class contests have very generally given way to intercollegiate struggles, we remember that '91 has always been well represented.

It would be wrong for me to omit a slight mention of the class contest of last fall, when by so close a margin '91 was victorious for the second time in general athletics. One lesson that strug- gle taught us—every point counts, and all honor is due him who, in the face of ridicule, finished every race and won for '91 the pennant.

Can any of us doubt that '91 has received lasting benefit from this hallowed ground? How well our temper has been curbed ; our nerves have been taught to remain steady, and our eyes have been trained to a clearness of discernment afforded by no other discipline. Have we more courage, think you, be- cause of our rushes ? Have we more determination to win, no matter what the odds may be ? These are the questions which each of us is to answer to the world. So much has been said of the close connection of brain and body that it is hard to say anything new on the subject, but we can say, though at times our scholarship may have suffered slightly, our hard and pains- taking work on this ground has fitted us to cope with the world far better than the mental discipline of many of our classroom recitations. A London member of the bar, on being asked the three requisites for a successful man, said, the first was a strong body, the second was a strong body, and the third was a strong body. Of what use is the man who breaks down ere his work has begun ? Life is a hard and long race, spasmodic efforts will not win it, pluck cannot always carry along the body, but the thorough training we have had in the coming battle will enable us to push steadily, strongly and surely to the front, to stand side by side with the strongest, and to show to the world, despite its scornful sneers, that he who worked on the miniature stage so steadily can stand the strain of severer strifes.

ADDRESS TO THE UNDERGRADUATES.

EDWARD WINGATE TEWKSBURY, WEST RANDOLPH, VT.

*F*ELLOW students:—Time and tide and the Chapel bell wait for no man.

Old father Time with sickle in his hand has hurried us on, and we stand to-day on the threshold of a busy world, bidding a fond, sad farewell to the scenes of our pleasant, happy college days.

> "Ah me! those happy days are gone,
> I little dreamt, until they were flown
> How fleeting was the hours."

Our college days are ended. No longer shall we frequent Dartmouth's classic halls, or sport upon the campus—the field of many a hard earned contest, or ramble in our beautiful park. All these we leave to you, fellow students, to you with whom we have been most pleasantly associated, with whom we have rejoiced over hard fought victories and have mourned over defeats. It is with a feeling of sadness that we go from these pleasant associations, yet we have joy and pride that we leave them in such worthy hands.

Old Dartmouth has won an honorable name—a name worthy of its illustrious founder, Eleazer Wheelock, who has reared a monument to his name more enduring than granite or bronze.

Old Dartmouth owes much to her alumni ; and I may also say her alumni owe still more to old Dartmouth. On you, also, fellow students, a great responsibility rests, that no action of yours in any way cast a blot upon Dartmouth's fair name.

Of all things be loyal to your *Alma Mater*. Be zealous in your studies. If you are a fraternity man aim to make your fraternity the banner one. In athletics aim to win, if you cannot win yourself cheer on the others. Aim in all things to keep Dartmouth's banner from trailing in the dust, and be ever ready to carry the "green and white" on to glorious victory !

Remember that the aim of a college education is to give a broad and liberal training as a solid foundation. Lay that foundation well! Then press onward and upward. Be ready to say with the old Roman, "*aut viam inveniam, aut faciam.*" Have a high ideal, so that in whatever occupation or profession you may choose in after life, that you may be an honor to your college, to yourself and to your God.

Our college course is ended. What is past is past. It is no longer ours. The race is still before you. Profit by our mistakes and avoid them. Press eagerly on to the goal and the reward will be yours.

'91 bids you a fond farewell.

CHRONICLES.

MARSHALL O. EDSON, WORCESTER, MASS.

S the writer has perused the finely written productions of preceding chroniclers he feels his incompetence to suitably portray the exploits of Ninety-one during the past four years. To this inability is added the scarcity of annual treatises containing sufficient data for this important work.

"Chang's" record of the events of Freshman year is a model one, and from its pages copious citations have been taken. The marked feature of "Goody's" Sophomore history was its peculiar phraseology, by reason of which it was deemed best that its publication be suppressed. "Pole cat" Willey, the commentator for Junior year, was too much engrossed in copying original editorials for the *Dartmouth* to attend to other business. His equivocal and misleading reply to the question when his effusion was to be delivered, " When the last chapter is written," proved very unsatisfactory. By some mistake no one was chosen to note the events of Senior year, so the field has been imperfectly covered.

The successful historian delineates his scenes in an attractive manner, regardless of slight discrepencies as to minor details. I have accordingly been actuated more by a motive to bring out salient points than to narrate in chronological order the records of all events as they have occurred.

Prex., in his opening lecture, gave us many valuable points regarding our future deportment and the brilliant career spread out before us. His speech was replete with many witty observations, and as we " wooded " his remarks to the echo—the upper classmen having given us a tip on this point—we must have made a good impression. This belief is confirmed by his participating with us in a foot-ball rush—the only instance of the kind on record. While watching the rare sport he was so overcome by the scenes and recollections of his earlier years that, putting aside for a time his customary dignity, he entered into the contest with a vim and enthusiasm which only a practiced adept could manifest. "Kit" Carson was inadvertently dragged from the *melée*, a performance "Kit" repeated the next year, when he pulled ont a classmate with much exertion and profanity, to the infinite delight of sundry Freshmen witnesses.

Willie P. Ladd was at once taken for a member of the Agricultural department, probably on account of his seedy looking moustache and the abstracted air he is accustomed to wear, indicative of deep meditation which might be directed upon the rotation of crops or scientific feeding. The soubriquet by which he used frequently to be known is suggestive of the affair.

Bryant caught on to "Tute" Lord's delivery in Greek, never striking out but frequently scoring a rush. This was before complications with the Western Union detracted from his skill. "Hoppy" early raised the point of illegal delivery on "Tute" Lord's part, and even insinuated, by his questions, that "Tute" did not know how to pitch. We all enjoyed the "mills," both for their own sake and for the opportunity given of translating ahead.

In the fall athletic meet "Pussy" Banfil essayed to contest with speedy Keay in the one hundred yards dash. The patronizing manner in which the latter "played horse" with him disgusted our youthful aspirant and he never again figured in athletic circles.

Eggleston came in second in the mile run. It may be mentioned in passing that there were but two contestants. It was decided that he should not again enter, as the sports could not begin in the forenoon.

C. F. Abbott wielded the boxing gloves with graceful ease, defeating his apponent without much difficulty; when it came to wrestling, however, the victor was not "in it" at all and measured his length on the ground with refreshing celerity.

The success of our tug-of-war team which defeated Ninety's men "Hoppy" has immortalized in verse. The team was composed of Doring, Bowles, Stanley and George. The victory created great enthusiam and was a just cause for pride. Such recognition was merited as it was one of the most brilliant events

of the year. In fact, it can be stated that our tug-of-war team
has never been defeated.

Pond and Carlton lost no time in impressing upon the den-
izens of Hanover that they came from a superior fitting school.
Walter's poorly appreciated yodels were frowned upon by the
roomers in Reed Hall, who could not stand the pressure. About
this time he was brought forward as a blushing bud into Hanover society, where some of its votaries have afforded him the
greatest happiness throughout his college course, except when
sundry Freshmen have got the start of him. It is currently reported that Pond had a good sized breach of promise suit on his
hands during his Freshman year. I have never heard the ru-
mor contradicted, and the affair was industriously hushed up.
Having been a former citizen of Lebanon his acquaintance per-
mitted him to get in his work before the rest of the boys. Now
"Watty," or even "Sandy," could give him points. The gen-
tleman from Haverhill gives us to understand his life has re-
peatedly been jeopardized by the shot gun of an enraged rival,
while the Lawrence letter carrier industriously circulates stories
of his own toughness, which are generally discredited.

They relate how Sam Holton, on his visit home, was the
object of much admiration from the fair sex. His best girl had
written him previously to be allowed to wear his society pin.
Sam pondered upon the pros and cons of this question long and
earnestly. On the one hand he would be pleased to gratify the
fair maiden as well as proud to see her thus arrayed ; on the
other he was undecided whether the cast iron oaths of the Alpha
Delts would allow such a departure. It is understood his personal leaning carried the day. Sam was, by all odds, the most
tired member of Ninety-one in consequence of the loss of the
menus at the class supper, for was he not sent in advance especially entrusted with their charge, and didn't he lose them on
his own stamping ground ?

"Chang" has graphically depicted in verse the adventure
of "Dave" Trull at St. Johnsbury. In brief the facts are these ;
J. Frank after sojourning for a season in Hanover, the desolate,
upon returning to his native heath wished to gratify the craving
of his social nature, while not averse to the public's knowing
the toughness he had acquired in a few weeks of college life.

An acquaintance divining his project and knowing his propensities dressed himself in female apparel with which he appeared upon the street. Frankie did not notice the deception and at once "caught on" and the tendencies of his fond and loving nature were manifesting themselves when the pseudo female could restrain himself no longer but burst into a laugh revealing his identity.

Early in his college course Tewksbury learned a practical lesson in regard to the capacity of the human stomach as well as on the evil of betting. Amazed at the amount of honey "Squash" got away with at a certain meal, the gormandizer offered to bet the price of the goods he could eat two pounds at one sitting. When this offer was accepted, the sweet stuff devoured with apparent relish while "Squash" sighed for more, the idea began to dawn on "Tewkie" that he was dealing with a future candidate for the spoon. "Tewkie" has not been known to hazard anything since, nor can he be induced to "set 'em up." Differing from the sponge in not allowing anything to be squeezed out of him, he is said to resemble that article in absorbing everything.

The joke played upon those who went out teaching is worth alluding to once more. The chief conspirators were Ladd, O'Brien and Bryant. "Tute" would have given them credit for possessing considerable information on the subject if they had shown themselves to be as well informed in recitation as they did in the examination paper they concocted and sent out to impose upon the unsuspecting pedagogues. It bore such a genuine appearance that all the victims readily fell into the trap with the exception of one or two who had some inside information.

Gilman received a call from the suffering people of North Thetford who suffered more than ever when he preached his last sermon. After matters had progressed swimmingly for some time, members of his flock were rudely awakened from the feeling of confidence they had reposed in their honored pastor. Some fair admirers came to see him in his own quarters in Thornton one beautiful spring day. All went merry as a marriage bell till some maliciously disposed associates in a neighboring room rapped at the door and returned the surprised B.

S. G. a tobacco box for the use of which they thanked him. "Humph" was the only exclamation which escaped him, but the visitors were horrified. While the party was on the streets taking in the sights, the conspirators regained possession of the box in which they placed a pipe and some tobacco. This was stealthily returned and afterward the guests carefully wrapped up the package to take home to exhibit to the natives as a tell-tale piece of evidence.

"Chang" was anxious to keep things humming and fomented considerable strife between Ninety and Ninety-one. Under his enthusiastic leadership the Sophomore class meeting was broken up by snow balls through the window, which resulted in the punishment meted out to certain ones in accordance with the verdict of "Heavy" Holmes. The decoy of the bogus telegram worked to a charm. The legend of brave Regulus on the bridge was reënacted. After jotting down the foregoing historic allusion I have considered who of the party most resembled Regulus. After mature deliberation I have reached the conclusion that "Freshie" Abbott deserves that distinction, first, because from his position among the rafters he was above everything base, and secondly because he remained at his post till all danger was over. Tommy who was entrusted with the class pipe, awoke one day to find his charge had walked off. Then Ninety's class histories came up missing. A brilliant idea again struck "Chang" and by the aid of a hectograph several copies advertising the loss were struck off and conspicuously posted.

Base-ball received early attention at our hands. "Watty's" proud boast that he had played three positions at once on his school team so paralyzed the fellows that he was chosen captain. Charlie Sibley claimed he could play as well as any man on the 'Varsity and so was made director. He officiated at one game as short stop. As every grounder batted in his direction bounded merrily past him, our phenom. concluded he was a trifle rusty in execution and retired. Willie P. Ladd was made manager, but having fallen asleep during a critical period of a game while keeping score it was decided a change must be made if victory was to perch on Ninety-one's banner. Accordingly Dan Richardson was chosen permanent manager for Freshman year.

It was thought his attractive looks would enlist the sympathies and admiration of the fair ones in the grand stand. While this result was effected it did not appear to be good policy as it gave the boys the "big head." When the time came for choosing Junior director the experience acquired was deemed valuable and it was resolved to select a plain looking person. DuBois was therefore elected, Sam Holton receiving first honorable mention and "Watty" second. The most interesting class affair in connection with base-ball was the trip to St. Johnsbury which has been dilated upon quite extensively in the class history. "Tute" Worthen had a little party in Culver that afternoon and much desired Dave Conant to stay and keep him company. Dave thought it would be decidedly uncivil to refuse the invitation and so was obliged to forego the pleasure of visiting his *alma mater.* The natives caught on to "Polly's" nickname and completely deranged his nervous system by distracting cries. Pond on his part tried to play a game of give away. The evening of that day was spent in various ways the most of which have been mentioned previously. One anecdote is worth recording which has been wrapt in oblivion thus far. "Watty" had seen some where a fascinating young lady of St. J. and was extremely anxious to meet her. He arranged with a friend to go with him to her residence and give him an introduction so that he might pass the evening pleasantly in a social visit. The presentation was made, "Watty" was delighted with the cordiality of his reception and looked forward to a most enjoyable evening. There was one disturbing element, however. This mutual friend was ignorant of the part he was to play, or else maliciously planned to dim the luster of the occasion. Instead of withdrawing at once, or after a short time, he seated himself to enjoy the interview. This was an unforeseen and unwelcome *denôument.* The conversation, forced into narrow and common-place channels finally lagged. "Watty" looked daggers at his friend(?), casting all possible expression into his eyes, still the hint was not taken. As another venture our hero inquired if he had any recitations the next morning. No, he had none. He did not go but stayed right there. Finally in desperation our classmate took a painful adieu, after which curses loud and deep fell on his companion for his stupidity.

Our Freshman history relates a most touching anecdote in which Dan Richardson figures as the hero. The story relates to a disappointment realized by him in not finding a girl he expected to when the ball team played at Lyndonville, and the breaking of an engagement at West Randolph. I hazard no opinion as to the basis of the report or the truthfulness of details.

Mr. Plummer for two years drove a flourishing trade in foot wear. To be sure his shoes would crack within a week and the rubbers were not much more reliable, but then, as Barnum said, "the American people like to be humbugged," and P. liked to humbug them. The climax of effrontery was reached when this merchant essayed to close a trade with Chase, the boot and shoe dealer, to hire rooms in his (Chase's) house for displaying Plummer's wares This appeared too much like heaping insult upon injury. Although several members of the class were in the habit of taking their Analyt. to the board to copy problem assignments, none were so bare-faced about it as our friend Plummer. It was extremely humiliating for him though not to be sufficiently acquainted with the problem he was at work on to apply what might be copied from the text. The researches of Ninety-one's Philosophical Club have doubtless exerted a more refining and elevating influence than almost any other organization in College. As a relaxation from too profound investigations, they indulged in a sleigh ride to Quechee last winter. By some fortuitous dispensation of fickle fortune Mr. Plummer was dumped into a snowdrift, where he was set upon savagely by a formidable member of the canine species. He suffered such a scare that he was unable to sleep for several nights.

About this time Rowe was performing the duties of assistant monitor. One Sunday, having repaired to church rather early and having marked several who were absent, "Chang" being of the number, he took the monitor's license of withdrawing. A few minutes later " Chang " arrived, gave Rowe a cut, and afterward, as he was head monitor, cancelled the mark against himself. The subordinate was evidently out generaled by his superior.

They tell of Pond committing the fatal blunder of stepping on a lady's foot while attending a ball at Lebanon. He did not

mend matters by the joking apology that he must step some-
where.

One of the first acts some of our classmates did to sig-
nify their acquisition of Sophomore toughness was to steal the
Freshmen's constitution. This was revised and adopted according to " Goody's " direction, printed and smuggled into Chapel,
where they were found next morning. " Hoppy " tried his hand
at writing poetry when he composed several verses challenging
the valor of the Freshmen. Some Ninety-two men, who tried
to emulate the Chapel affair, had a practical illustration of poor
dog Tray's fate.

" Chang " and " Dave " started out Sophomore year to coin
money hand over fist. The " Dartmouth Educational Bureau "
was carried on by competent managers. It was necessary that
the business should be lucrative. In the first place, the boys
were " stuck " in buying the concern, the fee simple, as the
" Dude " would phrase it. Again, after " Chang " had exhausted his own large vocabulary of gushing words and phrases for
his circular announcement he hired Barnum's agent to coach
him in the art, while " Dave " squandered all the prize money he
received in the district school for excellence in scholarship for
stationery and postage in soliciting business of school commit-
tees. The old dodge was worked for all it was worth, quite often successfully. " Chang," or " Dave," as the case might be, engaged the school for himself, was sick or had a broken leg and
sent a substitute. " Dave " became the successor of that worthy
pioneer, Chris. Anderson, in the furniture business. The good
will of that eminent philanthropist was bequeathed as a precious
heirloom, together with other damaged goods. " Dave " had that
same *suave* and confidential bearing, but probably did not have
that comprehensive grasp of vast enterprises. Chris.'s grasp of
his own affairs and those of others was something phenomenal.

While the presidential campaign of 1888 was at its height
political feeling ran high in college and different ones wagered
a considerable on their favorites. Tom Bailey was so sanguine
of Cleveland's winning that he put up a large sum on the result,
congratulating himself that he would have a snug sum to blow
in for the rest of the year. It is needless to say that he was
hopelessly left on that score.

Carleton had a pretty fairly well settled idea that in the musical line the Glee Club was about the stuff, especially the warbling. Imagine what a revulsion of feeling he must have had after the following incident. At a West Lebanon reception Walter inquired of a Fem. Sem., who did not know him, her opinion of the Glee Club. With artless simplicity she replied, she "liked the singing fairly well, but the warbling was just horrid."

Eggleston has had various railroad experiencs. Visiting a country school once to call upon the teacher he stayed too long and lost his train. This delay occasioned some embarassment. An another time he demanded a half-fare ticket of the station agent at Windsor without showing his certificate. The agent was suspicious, demanded to see his passports, and examining the certificate "Eggie" produced somewhat closer than he otherwise would haqe done. It proved to be dated the year before, and the agent pocketed the certificate and demadded full fare.

Sophomore class supper was accompanied by some striking scenes. Ninety-two, or that portion of the class which remained in town throug thought it would be a real smart act to abduct our genial toast-master. A sleigh stopped in front of Reed Hall early on the evening of the banquet and a dozen valiant Freshmen filed up the stairs to "Hoppy's" room. The omnipresent "Sailor" Cook, who nexer failed to be in the convenient proximity in a time of emergency, confronted the party with a drawn knife. With clenched teeth he threatened the first man who attempted to pass him. At this crisis J. Abbott, *demi dishabile*, appeared from his room on the scene. The mob abashed at the display of valor fell back dismayed, and when the hurrying feet of Ninety-one's reinforcements were heard on the stairs, took precipitous flight. After a most successful banquet at the Junction the celebrants of Washington's nativity set out and on their return, bound on further sport before the affair was ended. The dignity of the class had been assailed. Swift justice should be meted out to the offending partties. A court of competent(?) jurisdiction was instituted and summons were issued for two alleged malefactors—one a denizen of Alpha Delta Phi hall, and the other of "Bed Bug," to appear before this august February tribunal. The door of the latter place was strong and for a long time resisted the assault of the attacking party; finally the oaken sinews yielded to " Squash's " sledge hammer blows and the sought-for was found. John Abbott and " Goody " officiated as the counsel for and against the accused. It may be an open question whether or not the court was prejudiced, at any rate, the prisoners were convicted without much hesitation, and the appropriate punishment administered. Following the fun came the reaction. The faculty, swelled with abnormal self-importance by the responsibility resting on them in consequence of the Prex's absence among the miners of California, thought it a favorable time to show their authority. A season of inquisition revealed the names of those present at the trial. All these were branded as unclean outcasts, submitted to the fiendish torture of probation. The greater part of the class was thus shown to be scoundrels of the deepest dye. "Goody," " Squash," " Elder," " Sailor," John and Nat. Abbott had exhausted themselves by overwork and it was deemed desirable by the faculty that a change of climaʒe should be afforded them. John established his headquarters at the beautiful village of Norwich. There he became a leading figure in social circles, and his superior mental attainments made his residence easily the center of intellectual activity. " Elder " sent the following characteristic dispatch to his home in Illinois:

" Faculty has declared four weeks vacation. Shall I go home? HORTON."

His parents did not think it advisable to take so short a vacation and so he remained. His health, however, did not improve, and as other symptoms of an alarming nature began to break out it was deemed best that he withdraw indefinitely from college. The remainder of the party went to their several homes, returning at the beginning of the next term, much improved it was hoped.

The class went through some queer antics at the beginning of their course of instruction in German. All felt sure the first exercise would be unnecessary and so refrained from attending, with the exception of two or three. It seemed to the class that if those two or three were in such need of additional instruction the others did not have, that an hour would be inadequate. " Sailor," by plugging the keyhole, gave the instructor an opportunity to drill them in the rudiments of *Deutsch.* After that the class attended regularly, and, laying aside facetiousness, it can be said the instruction we received at the hands of Mr. Lord was excellent. Rowe neglected to give tne class cuts for being absent, in consequence of which his official head was taken off.

" Tommy " has worked the speech impediment racket for all it was worth and thus avoided some unpleasant labor. In the same way " Goody " has urged his physical disability upon the attention of the faculty, when anything was to be gained by it, as an absence from an unwelcome exercise. " Hoppy " showed his appreciation of physical strength when in the horn rush he gently asked a Ninety-three man, " Mr. Folsom, have you a horn about you ? " Receiving a reply in the affirmative, " Hoppy " rejoined, " All right then, I didn't mean to insinuate anything, you are a better man than I am and you may keep it."

The incidents attending the secession of Junior fall are fresh in our minds. " Prex " wore out one pair of shoes scurrying over town, conferring with his colleagues. The college gas bill was perceptibly increased, owing to protracted faculty meetings. John Proctor was privately reprimanded and exhorted for leaving the chapel organ, while " Freshie," in a burst of confidence, declared he " cared more for that ——— girl than all the colleges in the country." We secured, as tangible results, eight unexcused absences, besides much valuable information regarding other colleges, and learned something of the foxy character of those we had to deal with.

About this time Pond was relieved from his arduous duties in the library. Marvin's nature did not harmonize with that of our sweetly smiling Sappho, who was thus deprived of his opportunity of cribbing stories for the *Dartmouth.*

When " Squash," " Sid." and some others of that gang, went for a stroll each one gave his name as Doring, much to the disgust of that slandered person. Speaking of " Sid.," recalls the fact that when living over Cobb's store he became on more than friendly terms with some of the neighbors across the way. How far that acquaintance progressed can be inferred from the quaint remark of a loquacious four year old : " I've kissed Sid. Walker, and so has my Aunt Lizzie."

Rowe got into the habit of Dodge(ing) out of town at every opportunity Orford. The mistress of Conant hall club, where he waited, thought it too much of a burden to compel him to work while he had such *pressing* engagements elsewhere, and relieved him from further responsibility in the matter. As "Tewkie" was a relative of the parties Rowe took him along for a Saturday *soirée*. T. evidently took it for granted that they should take their departure about ten P. M., but R. did not have any such design. The evening spent pleasantly in conversation and games, at length wore on till a very late hour. T. began to gap, rub his eyes, and wonder why the other man did not have sense enough to take a hint. R. chattered on till one o'clock Sunday morning, and then was ready to catch the night train, to the infinite relief of T., who learned the distinction between one who is indifferently and one who is differently affected by the charms of certain female society.

While John Proctor and 'Wattie" were embarked for a voyage on the river they lost control of their boat, which capsized in mid stream. After some difficulty they regained their boat, when John found his watch was gone, which article was at length recovered. The pleasure of the occasion had vanished. Nothing like a thorough drenching will sober a man, no matter in how good spirits he may be.

A mean trick was played on Sam Holton, when he was made to carry a valise loaded with bricks from Norwich station to the village. Later he retaliated on Tom Bailey in a similar manner.

Speaking of Bailey recalls an anecdote in which he figured as the man who "got left." As he left for home he chanced to meet on the train before it reached the Junction a lovely young girl. Here was a chance for a delightful *tete-a-tete*, at the thought of which Tom hugged himself in a transport of ?oy. When the Junction was reached he proposed that they take a parlor car, which offer was accepted with thanks. A season of delicious enjoyment ensued, till the conductor coming along maliciously tore from Tom's mileage the fare for two, in spite of his vigorous protest, and would not make the matter right. However, this was but a slight matter, which our friend resolved should not take all the interest out of the occasion. He accompanied his fair companion clear to Boston. For some time he built airy castles as to what would be the outcome of this flirtation. His hopes were rudely dashed to the ground when he learned later that that she was engaged and was at very time on her way to the "Hub" to purchase her wedding outfit.

It will be remembered Junior fall that "Squash" was reported to have suffered a severe injury to his leg in foot-ball practice, preventing him from going with the team, and compelling him to limp about town with much difficulty. The true inwardness of the case is as follows: "Squash," with two or three wicked accomplices, had been over to Norwich for turkeys. The roost was reached without much difficulty and a fine bird was quickly under our hero's arm. But the fowl had uttered a cry before "Squash" had firmly encircled its neck. At once the watch dog set up a prolonged howl. Our friend lost no time but took leg bail for security. The night was dark, and he was unacquainted with the topography of the country. Hastening away with rapid strides he ran smash into a stone wall. Accustomed by Rugby practice to overcome all obstacles, the wall gave way, and so did "Squash's" knee. This is the explanation of the painful accident "Squash" alleges he received on the campus. The mysterious symbols T_1, T_3, T_5, which were current at that time related to the number of turkeys that could probably be obtained at certain designated places.

John "Crickett" Sanborn has at various times labored for Uncle Sam in the capacity of mail carrier. A close examination will reveal a deformity as a result of this employment in carrying one shoulder somewhat higher than the other. All the muckers and street urchins of Lawrence were on to "Sandy's" shape and created a lively diversion for him. John was willing to take all the chaff "Roots" saw fit to give him in Greek, and so got first prize. As "Jack" Wright was the only remaining one eligible for second place he thought he had a sure thing on that, but for some reason failed to arrive at his destination.

Many of the class have distinguished themselves as instructors of the youth. Echos from the schoolroom have occasionally been wafted back to Hanover. Willey, in Western Vermont,

became enamored of a blooming young widow, and that
teaching experience was one mass of sweetness long drawn
out.

Carleton, while engaged in didactic labors in Springfield,
Vermont, used to parade the streets every evening with a blushing maiden. "Goody" presided at Post Mills, to the infinite
delight of all the urchins who attended school. Great sorrow
was expressed when the term was over, as they could not remember having everbefore enjoyed such a picnic. Prichard,
while keeping school, had the unmitigated gall to teach Greek,
although he had never studied the subject. By judicious plugging, supplemented by ready conversational powers and an as-
sumption of owl-like wisdom, he got along very well and was
considered very proficient in the subject. Warren is said to
have sufficient nerve while teaching to employ his time in school
plugging his college work. Doring's foot-ball experience ena-
bled him to lay flat three or four strapping fellows, who essayed
to try titles with him. They entertained a wholesome respect
and admiration for the game of Rugby thereafter.

The presentation of Junior honors was a noteworthy event
in the history of the class. "Hoppy," in flaming handbills, had
exhausted his stock of startling headlines. It was truly a red
letter day for this brilliant scion, and his efforts in making the
event a success were duly appreciated. Each event was adver-
tised in a striking manner, appropriate to the occasion. The
speeches were all good and appreciated. Barton, as he received
the petticoat, turned the tables nicely on Sid. Walker. Gilman
made a very witty speech in presenting the nursing bottle to
Tewksbury. "Slugger" illustrated the use to be made of a pil-
low, but Watson felt to much the chagrin of presenting the mir-
ror to say anything. Plummer made a happy hit in observing,
as he received the salt cellar, that the remarks of the presentist
should be taken *cum grano salis.* One of the features of the evening was the dissemination of mysterious circulars, entitled
the "Asses Symposium." The cast of characters comprised
"Chang," "Kid," "Goody," "Hoppy," and "Sid." The Fe-
line quartet was composed as follows:

First Howler,   Cuteness Barrows.
Second Screecher, Alpha Pussey Banfil.

3

First Croaker,   Tom Cat Bailey.
Second Bellower,   Pole Cat Willey.

Following this was given a synopsis of the play, which it is unnecessary to give here, suffice it to say, the hits were well
appreciated and created much merriment.   The design was evidently to grind the *Ægis* board in anticipation of their produc-
tion.   Common consent has ascribed this remarkable piece of
literary work to " Slugger," aud he has not been known to deny
the soft impeachment.

The tardy appearance of the *Ægis* created some diversion
and speculation.   It was supposed to have been kept back on
account of its radical and objectionable character.   This belief
was enhanced by the fact that some of the board had work to
make up and they were anxious to get square with the board
and also as they expected to be fired for the rest of the year, by
waiting till the last moment, their period of banishment would
be as short as possible.   When the long expected appeared be-
hold how harmless a thing it was !   " Prex " is said to have
smiled as he read " Hasten the day," John K. went into ecsta-
cies over " Noah's Ark, " while " Clothes-pin" pronounced
" Much ado about nothing " a gem among literary burlesques
and of high artistic merit.   The take-off on " Scratchy Dave "
was a hard one and ground the person interested as much as
it delighted the public at large.

" Tewkie " has been the victim of many interesting experi-
ences.   That bit of romance when he savagely struck " Beans "
with the angry adjuration " Wake up, Susan " pales into insig-
nificance in comparison with an exciting ride last summer vacation.   While going through some enterprising evolution, he
had the misfortune to plunge head foremost down between the
cross-bar and axle.   His feet naturally could not pass through
this orifice, and there he hung suspended 'twixt heaven and
earth.   No horse of any *animus* could be indifferent to such a
performance so he accordingly ran at the rate of five miles an
hour, more or less, with poor " Tewkie " in perilous danger.
Dirty, bruised and bleeding, he was at last rescued and it required the rest of the vacation to recuperate for college in the
fall.   He mourned long and loud over the destruction of a sev-
enty-five cent straw hat.

Heath was supposed to have spent last summer vacation surveying out West. Inside advices state he was driving mules as a business and only surveying the landscape. " Birdie " who drove the mules?

Ladd as treasurer of the Y. M. C. A. proposed to drive a sharp bargain in getting the Student's hand-book of information printed. After the trade was made and the work completed, Willie began to beg off, stating the price agreed upon was much too high and the work was unsatisfactory. He pathetically wrote how he cried with disappointment when the work was received, hoping to secure a big discount. The gag did not work and when the printer threatened suit Willie came to time like a little man and settled the bill.

In Political Economy, Bailey in reply to the question what the lowest form of employer is called replied " The Boss. " Tom always had a voluble flow of language while reciting, reminding one of Hippias who " could say something new on any subject at any time." The originality of his remarks was often striking. " Dude " asked George his opinion if the state should legislate to deprive all persons having pink eyes from certain privileges. With surprising wit Guy replied " it would be a discrimination against color.

Prichard showed considerable *finesse* in recitation. Sitting on the front seat, that sardonic grin would disappear as " Dude " called him up and he would give the most respectful attention to the queries propounded to him. To a series of leading questions " Prich " instead of replying " yes," would say " It is " in a low tone of voice. When the " Dude " would twist about in his chair squinting sideways through his glasses, indicating either that the answer was wrong or he did not understand, " Prich " assuming the latter would repeat " It is not " in an off-hand way. If the " Dude " was known to have a sense of the humorous we should have supposed he was making a personal allusion when he asked of Burbank in connection with Federal appropriations for rivers and harbors if Sugar river was navigable for anything but row boats. How the " Jew " blushed.

" Gabe " can never resist the chance for a joke. In this respect he is nearly as bad as " Prex." Cobb in reciting on Socrates stated that at forty years of age he appeared in the clouds. "Yes" retorted "Gabe," "and at seventy he went higher." "Gabe" made the ruling that all who received a recitation mark of 80 % should be exempt from examination. The way he chose those to take the exam. must have been like placing the names in a box, shaking them up and drawing out, blind-folded a certain number. He allowed the "Kid" to get through Psychology by a narrow squeeze, but afterward his conscience must have troubled him as he made him take an exam. in Philosophy although he had done excellent work. "Kid" was prepared for emergencies however and a sheet of paper inside his cuff made his deficiency exam. a howling success. Four men started out in the course of Hebrew. Willey found out it looked too much like work, "Jack" Wright saw he could not keep on and draw out more than ten novels a day from the library. while Banfil dropped it in order to have time to take the course of dancing lessons. Thus Fish is the only one left who can speak fluently in Hebrew.

Burbank left his gas jet open last winter vacation and on returning found charged to his account two hundred feet. Bailey and Holton combined could not supply that amount in talk. The contest between Sargent and Plummer is worthy of note. The former was at work night and day to excel in Practical Chemistry researches, while the latter changing his results to conform to the right answers held him a close second. The unequal conditions under which they competed resembled the fabled race between the tortoise and the hare.

Colby delighted "Chuck's" heart by his fine work in Physics in recognition of which the instructor has rewarded him with the degree of "Doctor of Results." If any one ever was handicapped in his desire to excel it was John Proctor. Being familiar with his proclivities from childhood up every disturbance occurring in the class room has been persistently laid at his door so his deportment has lowered his standing to quite an extent.

One day last fall Gilman set out from White River Junction to walk to Hanover. Absorbed in one of Phillips Brooks' sermons which he intended to spring on his flock the next Sunday, he gave no attention to the bridges he was crossing or the direction he took. After a season of meditation he looked up to find himself in Hartford. Having edified the people of Thetford for nearly three years he was compelled to go; the specific counts in the indictment were that he wore light clothes, rode a bicycle and refused to kiss the babies. He claims his success at Lyme as a vindication of these charges.

Kibbey has held forth at Tunbridge, Vermont to the surprise and delight of his hearers. The people would not believe his sermons original. His bland and child-like appearance doubtless gave rise to the suspicion of plagiarism. Among his regular auditors was our friend Bugbee. It may seem strange to the uninitiated that he should go so far to attend divine worship. The fact is Bugbee has lived in Tunbridge more or less for the past four years and it seemed real homelike to attend church there. An item appearing in the *Dartmouth* a few weeks ago to the effect that " Kibbey, '91, had been spending a few days visiting friends in Tunbridge, Vermont," shows his sojourn there has not been in vain. Kibbey mistakenly ascribed this squib to Bugbee and the next issue of the *Dartmouth* contained the information that " Bugbee, '91, had been spending a few days visiting friends in Tunbridge, Vermont." Honors are now easy. Bailey and Heath purported to be employed in a Boston book store as salesmen last winter. A friend called to see them but the head salesman did not know any such names. Questioning a ragged striker of the establishment he was shown into a dark, dirty cellar where our heroes were found in old clothes and sleeves stripped industriously engaged, one in washing windows, the other shaking ashes.

In the future a picture of " Hoppy " seated in his office, will recall a familiar scene and suggest many incidents of old times. He and the parrot became sweet confidants. The parting was grievous, and neither could be reconciled to the cruel irony of fate. " Tewkie " once was taken violently ill and consulted Dr. Chapman. After a critical diagnosis " Chappie " gave him a lecture on hygiene and prescribed some pills to be taken. Soon after the Doctor sent in a bill of fifty cents. Upon an itemized bill being demanded it was explained that twenty-five cents were for the pills and twenty five for the advice. "Tewkie " paid the quarter for pills, and with characteristic meanness told " Chappie " he might keep his advice to himself.

Cobb, while having charge of his domestic heating arrangement, last fall, allowed the hot water to flood the chambers. In consequence, he was busily employed for some time in carrying down stairs bucketfuls of water, a work for which he was admirably adapted by nature.

Carleton and his Glee Club aggregation were nicely "pulled" last winter. The. U. M. team, "all in full dress suits," having tried unsuccessfully to hire a certain hall in Barre, secured another. The proprietor of the first, not to be outdone, hired Carleton's troupe for the same night and billed the town thoroughly to draw from the U. V. M. concert. Having succeeded in this very well, and having no further use for the Dartmouth crowd, he wired them not to come, as they had reached the Junction en route for Barre. A crest fallen crowd returned back to town a little later.

Ninety-one has always been conspicuous in chapel. Fish is said to have been the first one to wood up "Hasten the day." "Slugger's" devotional character has frequently been noted. John Proctor used to play the latest skirt dance for voluntaries. "Billy" Bailey got tired of singing in the choir one Sunday night and started to take his seat. The look of blank surprise he gave on turning about and seeing the rest retain their positions was not lost on the audience. The note "Jack" Wright was about to strike could be determined accurately by observing the height his eyebrows were raised.

In one of Gilman's eccentric moods for which he is noted he conceived the idea that a type writer was what he wanted and must have. A letter was accordingly written to a dealer in New York stating his need and asking for prices and other information concerning the different styles of machines. This was sent to the chairman of the church committee, Newbury, Vermont. The communication intended for the latter party in regard to supplying their pulpit was sent to the type writer agency in New York. The good people of Newbury were shocked beyond expression to find the prospective theologian should think of indulging in such an expensive luxury as a type-writer, while the New York concern is doubtless still looking for a vacant pulpit for our classmate. It may be observed that on another occasion a letter of his intended for a classmate reached a young lady, while the letter destined for the y. l. was received by the c.

Last winter " Birdie " chanced to see in an agricultural paper a prize offered to any one who should combine the letters of a given word so as to form the largest number of words. With a zeal worthy of a better cause " Birdie " diligently perused Webster's unabridged and sent a thousand words more or less. No prize was forthcoming but in a few days our hero received a communication from a party evidently taking the person addressed for a bright, wide-awake and enterprising farmer's son

" BRATTLEBORO, VT., March 2, 1891.

A. C. HEATH, Hanover, N. H.

We have no agency for our Food in your town and would like to have you take hold of it. The profit is large and you run no risk, as we guarantee the Food to prove satisfactory and as represented, or we will refund the purchase money. Please read the testimonials in our circulars from prominent horse and cattle owners, some of whom you know.

We make oath that Peel's Condition Food contains nothing injurious to man or beast.

March, April and May being the best months in the year for the sale of condition foods and powders, we hope you will send us a trial order at once and place it before your customers. Remember that it costs nothing unless it proves as represented. We could not afford to sell poor goods on these terms.

Yours respectfully,   PEEL'S FOOD COMPANY."

" DuBy " has always been noted for unmitigated gall and supreme nerve. On one occasion he attended a party at Norwich where he became charmed with the society of an attractive companion. After taking her to supper he requested the pleasure of escorting her home. Upon the young lady expressing her regrets that she had accepted the invitation of another fellow, Charles assumed an injured air saying that as he had taken her to supper he expected of course to see her to her abode. The potent argument that a quarter of a dollar spent in her behalf placed her under obligations proved too strong, and the base-ball magnate won his point. " DuBy " and Dan

have been threatened with legal prosecution for violation of the
game laws of Vermont by hunting Partridges on Sunday and
and during the moulting season.

"Polly" has distinguished himself as the valiant champion
of democratic principles as opposed to the church oligarchy

As the mild Spring days came on "Goody" and "Hoppy"
sighed for a relaxation from severe mental toil, so one day
they embarked for White River Junction for a little recreation.
After a day's outing they set out on their return taking the six
o'clock train.   Not a cloud dimmed the sky of their happiness,
their hearts were light and free, they were in the best of spirits
and everything seemed bright to them.   It seemed therefore
incumbent upon them to do something bright.   When the train
reached Norwich "Goody" took up a box of cigars belonging
to the train boy while "Hop" took several novels under his
arm, and the two with much dignity seated themselves on the
top of Howe's coach.   Just as the train was about to start the
vender missed his goods, looked out to see them and had just
time to climb on the rear end of the coach as it drove away.
His equanimity was somewhat disturbed at seeing his Havanas
dispensed with a lavish hand and he threatened dire vengeance.
Meanwhile the maurauding pair began to have grave doubts as
to the feasibility of their undertaking.   When the Wheelock
was reached "Goody" took a hasty circuit about the college
buildings and esconsed himself safely in his own room.   "Hoppy" likewise departed in another direction, reached the mouth
of Mink brook, took a boat to a place opposite the Vale of
Tempe where he remained until some associates found him.
His voice was highly tragic as he exclaimed in a sepulchral
tone "My name is Hopkins, and I'm a fugitive from justice."
Only $10 was required to meet the exsenses of such an amount
of fun.   In the balmy month of May, Sargent one Sunday asked Stanley to walk to Lyme with him.   The latter not to refuse
a challenge consented to go although he dreaded the walk proposed.   They sallied out, walking on the Vermont side the first
of the journey, and on this side returning.   The dust was unpleasant while the heat was intolerable.   Neither the beauties
to please the eye or the ear at length seemed to delight them
and the journey became one horrid grind.   At length footsore

and hungry they reached Hanocer after a walk of 20 miles and if anyone mentioned Lyme to Stanley for several days after he did it at his own risk.

If there is anything that "Jack" Wright prides himself in it is his critical knowledge of literature. Consequently, when "Clothespin" asked, in an examination, something about Hawthorne, this lad felt called upon to free his mind as follows: "Who is this Hawthorne? Some old woman's writer. Some poor, dissolute, inconsequential scribbler of weak prose." This frank expression of opinion is said to have endangered his chances for final honors, besides knocking away his last show for the general improvement prize. Ninety one was well represented and acquited itself with much credit at the Springfield meet. Although the Amherst sprinter won the quarter mile run he acknowledged he had a hard row(e) to hoe. The judge got in a cruel thrust on "Eggie" when announcing the result of the two mile run he stated the third man had not yet been heard from. Every one felt sorry for Doring whose unfortunate accident undoubtedly deprived us of the tug-of war. No one has trained more faithfully, or commanded more the confidence of the fellows than he, and all felt the disappointment to him to be greater than their own. "Squash," by the magnificent way he threw the hammer, added to the honor he had already won as the most satisfactory athletic manager the college has had for years. Our friend George received the following comment in the Springfield *Republican*: "One of the funniest exhibitions of the afternoon was that of George of Dartmouth in putting the shot. Tall, round shouldered, his arms twich as if with the ague as he prepares to make the lurch."

Barton went out botanizing, on one occasion, in the outlying districts. A farmer's inquiry if the Dean had returned showed that Mr. B. had been taken for a member of the department about to remove to Durham. Carson Smith had a similar experience when the Chandler men began their course in Mineralogy. "Type" was not at all familiar with the faces of the subjects he had to deal with, for when Carson entered the room he was peremptorily told that "this is the Chandler Scientific class." Carson blushed a beautiful scarlet tinge, and stammered confusedly as he endeavored to impress upon "Type's"

mind that he was not a member of the College of Agriculture
and the Mechanic Arts.

On the Amherst base-ball trip Heath attempted to kiss a
waiter girl. At this critical juncture her false teeth fell out,
which checked his mad impulse. They tell of "Tommy's" en-
tering the Connecticut river bridge, thinking he was going into
the livery stable, one dark night. "DuBy," "Tewkie," and several under classmen, used to compete for the society of a certain lady at White River Junction, with varying success. "Du-
By" went to the Junction one night to attend an entertainment,
and posted himself near a certain house from whence he conjec-
tured she would shortly appear. After a time she did appear,
but as she was accompanied by another fellow, Charles felt cha-
grined and passed a miserable evening. John Abbott attended
the same show, and essayed to do the manly thing by escorting
a girl home. She proved decidedly young and unsophisticated,
for as they left the hall she called back, "O mamma, are not you
coming too?" John had not taken the contract of looking out
for the family, but his friends appreciated the scene immensely.
He was so enraged when their school paper touched him up on
the matter that he refused to sing with the class choir, jumped
with both feet on every one who had not paid his *Dartmouth*
subscription, and fired two men from the 'Varsity.

Such, classmates, is an imperfect record of the humorous
events which have transpired during the four years of our college course. When the review of our lives is written may the
record of each member of the class stand forth, bright with glorious achievements and crowned with success and happiness.

PROPHECIES.

BY FRED ELMER PRICHARD, BRADFORD, VT.

"The best prophet of the future is the present."

Y inclinations are not as sulphurous as those of the prophetic prodiges who have preceded me ; in fact I am decidedly opposed to a close acquaintance with burning brimstone, therefore for this occasion I have not, like them, taken any trip to Hades to look for the future of '91. I do not imagine the mantle of a Moses or a Samuel has fallen upon me, nor do I like the older prophets disclaim all ability to quote the poets, for there is one in our class whose influence is not to be forgotten.

But with all the reality of this occasion the surrounding scene is a new one to us. The green hills that circle the paths where "Sandy" and "Wattie," Woodcock and Allison used to wander to watch the occultations of the stars and enjoy, with some village maidens, the osculations of the lips ; the summer house where Thompson spent many an hour with the girl it would not be "proper" for him to have present on this occasion—these things have passed away. All recollection of them is absorbed in Marshall O. and those acursed chronicles of his, in which he hurled the red hot irons of his infamous wrath at forty-six of the purest men that ever suffered martyrdom. But

"His tongue is now a stringless instrument,
Words, life, substance and all old Pluto hath spent."

"There is a history in all men's lives,
Figuring the nature of times deceased ;
The which, observed, a man may prophesy,
With near aim, of the main chances of things
As yet not come to life, which in their seeds,
And weak beginnings, lie intreasured."

It required no especial gift to prophecy the life of Ferda Fish. He passed through Hartford Theological Seminary, after gaining the respect and affection of a quiet country parish, he spent the greater part of his life as a foreign missionary, a work for which he had been preparing for several years, commencing at *Dartmouth College* with Charlie Sing & Co. The good he did can never be estimated.

Kibby and Gilman continued to fill the pulpit and the latter found a parish more congenial to his taste than Thetford, where he could wear a tennis suit and ride a bicycle to his hearts content and was not expected to kiss all the babies in the community.

Messrs. Barnard, Walker & Hopkins started for a tour with their "Greatest Show on Earth" and rivaled the reputation of A. Ward's Museum of Arts. They continued their prosperous career till "Hoppy" became a "fugitive from justice" and then gave up the business. "Hoppy" studied law and in time equalled his father as a champion of woman's rights and a dispenser of justice. "Kid" returned to Franklin after the dissolution of the firm where he continues to live on the reputation and property of the Judge, his father. "Sid" entered the Thayer School. His reputation as an engineer is equalled by few and surpassed by none.

Herr E. Wingate Tewksbury may be found any day at A. W. Tewksbury's emporium, whose sign has been displaced by one reading E. W. Tewksbury, A. B., Dealer in Fine Feed and Groceries. Nevertheless "Tewkie" is happy and has realized his idea of bliss—a small house, a pretty wife, a bath tub and a fire place.

"Goody" followed the wishes of his friends rather than his own desires when he entered the ministry. He still continued to maintain the high standard of morals he had established in college.

"Hard Luck Dave" after graduation, helped the good deacon on the farm for a year or two, then at the earnest solicitation of the faculty and trustees accepted the chair of Moral Philosophy in Dartmouth College. The way he requests men to look their notes over a little more far excells that of his worthy predecessor.

"Birdie" Heath, "Wattie" and Warren represented '91 in D. M. C. Heath and Watson became typical "medics," but Warren hadn't the moral courage and succumbed at the end of the first year and took up teaching with much better success.

Hazen accepted the position of instructor in Mathematics and Greek in Kimball Union Academy, where he soon secured the principalship. There he bids fair to spend his life.

"Chang" the wily man, studied law, a profession for which he was admirably adapted. The reputation he established as a criminal lawyer is to be envied, but alas! he did not follow the example of Abraham Lincoln for he doesn't care whether his client is innocent or not, in fact I think he preferred the guilty party so long as he had money, for it gave wider scope for his psycological puzzles.

John Proctor, after acting as Prof. Emerson's assistant for a while, traveled with Prof. Young to enlarge his knowledge of Astronomy. When he returned he concluded with Solomon that "all the labor of his hands which he had labored to do was vanity and that there was no profit under the sun," also that "there is nothing better for a man than that he should eat and drink" and smoke straight cuts, so he settled down to enjoy himself.

"Sandy," the agnostic, served Lawrence in the capacity of mail-carrier to the great satisfaction of the patrons. He concluded, after a time, that a man that "knew he didn't know anything" ought to do more for the human race than to distribute mail to a small fraction of it, accordingly he established a school for agnostics, which rivaled those of Athens and Rome.

C. F. Abbott, the man of great possibilities, who could have been on the 'Varsity, if he would only train," to say nothing of the one hundred yards dash and half-mile race he might have won at Springfield if he had wanted to, after a little struggle with the inconsiderate people of a small western town, concluded that potentiality didn't pay and settled down to business in the political arena, where he gained great glory, finally standing at the head of our diplomatic corps at London.

Allison, Willey and Wright established world-wide reputations as critics of German, French and English, respectively. Wright finally secured the position of Prof. of Anglo-Saxon and

English Literature in a Western University, where for the first time he learned to answer his own question, " Who is this man Hawthorne ? "

Rowe worked for the Springfield Republican as a reporter till he had become proficient as a journalist, then started a paper for himself which became the official organ of the Farmers' Alliance so insuring its success during the mushroom like growth of that party.

Banfil continued to read service at Littleton where he en· tertained the people with accounts of the advantages of rooming on Faculty Avenue, and becoming acquainted with Professors families. You may find his latest work, "Society as I Found It" in Hanover, on the counter of every large bookstore in the country.

Barton became a naturalist as was expected. He succeeded Prof. Hitchcock and became as typical of the Eozoic Age as the original type.

Burbank settled in Claremont. He lives a quiet life, in this mecca of the reserves, as principal of the high school.

Bugbee and George became successful teachers. Bugbee making a specialty of Psychology and George of Greek and Putting the Shot.

Holton and Bailey went into the coal and insurance business in Hanover. " Sammy " finding that there was too much for one to do took Bailey into partnership with him. It is needless to say they lived comfortably on the profits.

Ladd found the " Old Pine Bookstore " such a source of income that he continued in the business and pushed Storrs to the wall and secured the monopoly of the student trade.

Pollens and Lord studied together in Germany and settled in Strasburg as instructor in English and French.

Plummer is still in the boot and shoe business at 92 Hanover St., Boston.

" Sluggard " continues the hard worker he always was.

Colby and DuBois are physicists of considerable merit, both finding positions in western colleges, where " DuBy " has recovered the losses sustained in the management of the 'Varsity.

Cobb is at the old stand in Hanover.

Carleton is his father's assistant at Bradford but according to rumors he devotes more time to the seminary than to the boys school.

Thompson never could stand excitement and late hours and may be found quietly settled in Concord, where a hearty welcome awaits any number of '91 who may visit that city.

Edson and Heald are to be found with Ginn & Co., as traveling agents.

Richardson and Trull could not part company after living together so long and concluded to make Norwich their home, where they became mighty sons of Nimrod. They still prefer Pattridges to all other Vermont game.

Little, the Webster cyclone, familiarly known as " Squash," returned in the fall to enter the Thayer School. Of course he had to play foot-ball and as a rusher had no equal. After finishing his two years in the post graduate course, he found a position as railroad engineer where he surveyed the road-bed in a way that rivaled Prof. Worthen's front line of the Y. M. C. A. building.

Stanley, and Carson Smith are in the law business. They meet with varying success, but mostly good.

" Kit " and " Doc " studied medicine and are settled in practice. " Kit " still vehemently declares the old school the best.

" Eggie " and Sargent are wanderers on the face of the earth, but for no bad purpose. There is a rivalry between them for the largest herbarium and they bid fair to wander their days out.

Your prophet has been unable to foresee anything definite in the matrimony line but if he can judge at all from the actions of Rowe and C. F. Abbott to-day he would think the class was not backward with the fair sex. He also knows of a wager that "Tewkie" marries inside of two years. The other cases are too numerous to mention and I will leave it to each to decide for himself whether marriage is a failure.

I am unable to say anything about the future of Prichard. His horoscope seems to indicate that a very stormy and critical period has arrived and there are doubts about his surviving more than fifteen minutes, however republics always were ungrateful.

ADDRESS AT THE TOWER.

GEORGE MARSHALL WATSON, HAVERHILL, N. H.

TRAVELERS tell us that amid the the ruins of an ancient city there remains a massive monolithic pillar, bearing characters in a strange and unknown tongue. Amid the surrounding desolation it stands solitary and alone, the silent reminder of events now lost to history.

To-day we dedicate *our* part of *this* granite tower, a silent yet expressive reminder of the events, the associations, the triumphs of our college life. And while it stands as the last mile stone along the way we have come, it also marks the beginning of another epoch in our lives, full freighted with new hopes and aspirations.

Perhaps to some the closing scenes of each class serve no useful purpose, and are but meaningless rites. To us they have a significance and a meaning tnat only the initiate can fully know. The erection of this tower is not alone a memorial to ourselves, but rather a mausoleum around which cluster these ties " that from the birth of lettered friendship rise." Other feet will tread the familiar way; other voices will echo within these gray and time-honored walls, but our class friendship will never grow dim—our love and labor for Old Dartmouth never cease.

Perceiving the events of the years that are now about to culminate, we discover many joys and few sorrows, thus gaining a new and a broader view of the life before us. Then with a purpose and ambition born of the years let us enter the lists and break a lance to a good purpose, for the goal *is* worthy of our best efforts.

> " Between two worlds life hovers like a star,
> 'Twixt night and morn upon the horizon's verge.
>
> How little do we know that which we are,
> How *less* what we *may* be."

Laying aside useless regrets for what we might do if we could recall the last four years, let our future quest be more light, more truth, more knowledge. Let us make some point in the yet unexplored field of science and thought, our objective aim. In the results, as measured by our efforts, will be the true test of character. As these different blocks of granite are firmly cemented together, so may the ties of friendship that bind us now, however distant we may be, keep us as in the past.

Far away beneath an oriental sky, surrounded by the beauties of a most luxuriant tropical vegetation stands the most beautiful structure of which modern archæologists have any knowledge. Built by a pagan Emperor of creamy marble, inlaid with gems and precious stones, and dedicated to the memory of an undying love. Beneath the ample dome pilgrims stand in rapt and silent admiration the while they ponder the inscription and drop a tear to the memory of the sleeping dust beneath. And as it rears its lofty shaft of spotless marble, cold and white, sharply outlined against the sky, it needs no poet to sing its praise, no pen to chronicle its history.

We consecrate this shaft to the memories we leave behind us, we gather around it as successive classes have done before us to pledge anew our vows of fidelity to our *Alma Mater.* When moss covered it shall have grown and forgotten shall be the forms that now gather around it, defying the winter storms and the summer heat, still let it stand the monument of our undying love.

ADDRESS AT THE OLD PINE.

FRANK W. PLUMMER, SOMERVILLE, MASS.

AND now, classmates, we come to the sad part of our day's exercises. Here, beneath the sheltering branches of the Old Pine, we gather as classes of old have done, to say good-bye. For four years have we assembled together, day by day, and as I look around me to day I miss the faces of some who gathered with our class on our first morning in college, and see others who have since joined us.

It is truly fitting, at this time, mayhap the last at which we as a class gather together, to pause a moment ere we part. For four years have we been building th s foundation, as it were, to our life, and now having reached the goal toward which our efforts have been directed from the day we entered Dartmouth, we call to mind our victories and defeats, our pleasures and sorrows but for a moment, absorbed as we are in the contemplation of what the future has in store for us.

Let us, as we part to go in different directions, strive for some rank in life wihich will bring credit to ourselves and honor to our class.

The general mass of mankind are satisfied with the conditions around them. Each rising and setting of the sun sees them beginning and ending the same work as on the day before, conforming to the same customs and usages of their fathers, with no thoughts of going beyond them, or of improvements for the minds and bodies of their fellowmen. All that has been accomplished in the past, whether in literature for the intellect of men, or for justice and humanity, were once but thoughts or theories in the minds of their authors. These were not obtained without struggles and sacrifices. Heroes have fallen and martyrs have died that freedom and truth might rise and live.

Energy of character was an important factor in the lives of such men, who struggled long to attain the one end they had

steadfastly in view. What noble examples we have of such energy in the lives of those in the past! And as we have found them
in the past we can still find them to-day and the morrow will
bring forth new ones.

It may not be the lot of any of us to fall in a strife for freedom or die a martyr in the cause of truth, yet we can take to
heart the lessons they have taught. While one needs a true esti-
mate and knowledge of his strength and ability, the mainspring
of success in life is *perseverence.* Peiseverence to remain firm,
through struggle and defeat, to the purpose of one's life is the
one important element to success.

And now, classmates, may the same friendship and har-
mony which has bound our class together in the past continue
until the final reunion day.

Do thou, Old Pine —Dartmouth's silent guardian—grant
success to the hopes, the aims and the efforts of each and every
one of Dartmouth Ninety one.

www.ingramcontent.com/pod-product-compliance
Lightning Source LLC
Chambersburg PA
CBHW031814090426
42739CB00008B/1263